The Bright Side of Death

A Journey into the Meaning of Life

Dario D'Angelo

DEDICATION

In loving memory of my brother Trung

CONTENTS

ACKNOWLEDGMENTS

To my beloved wife Tina for all the support and help with the
excruciating editing of my Italian-English. To Kin Lau for his
motivational push and the great work in creating the cover. To
Amanda Byma and Ted Mawla for their careful review and
suggestions. It maybe a very small step for mankind,
but it is surely a great leap for me.
Thank you.

CHAPTER ONE

THE ELEPHANT IN THE BOOK

First things first. Why write a book about death? It is not to become rich, as you may be reading the only copy I will ever sell. It is not to dump my emotional baggage on a computer hard drive to appease my shrink. And believe me when I say that despite my sociopathic nature, I do not intend to sadden you, nor to convince you of anything I believe in.

The main reason why I wrote this book is so that I can appear on *The Colbert Report* at least once. Before you jump to any conclusion, it is not because I want fame, glory and fortune – but rather, just fame. I am not even asking for the traditional 15 minutes; ten minutes and the *"Colbert Bump"* will do it.

As a self-proclaimed "aspiring comedian," this would be as close as I could get to success.

Keep in mind that an interview with "The Rev. Sir Doctor Sen. Stephen T. Mos Def Colbert, D.F.A., Heavyweight Champion of the World**, Ph.D" is no easy task, and I do not take the challenge lightly. Years of preparation are needed. You must have a couple of copies of the United States Constitution, an ability to ignore verbal domination, and the assertiveness to simply impose your point of view if, or rather when, you get interrupted.

If you still do not understand my motive or do not appreciate this hilarious *Comedy Central* show, that's on you.

At times I've questioned my ability to write anything, let alone write in English. An Italian immigrant, with English as a second language, computer science as background, and with a laughable sense of humor only a wife can appreciate (I know it is because she loves me…despite the meals), and with the words of my friend Sean always in my mind ("You are not funny; I am!"), my chances of succeeding have felt like zero.

Until, one day – by accident – I noticed a book by one of my comedy heroes: Denis Leary's *Merry F***IN' Christmas*. Suddenly I felt… empowered. I must confess that I was not one of the five people who bought it; I just "read" its 32 pages at the book store, as I could not swallow paying twelve bucks for it. But anyway, the point is this: if that "book" can be published, then anything can. If Denis Leary can write books, so can I!

A warning for those who are sensitive to sensitive people like me: inevitably there are a few chapters forthcoming that are not too cheerful. You must allow me some slack here, as the subject ain't easy. Beyond that, you are the one who chose to read a book with this title. Find consolation in the fact that at least you did not pay \$12 for it.

Even if contemplating the inevitable is arguably a waste of time, your personal life could benefit from it. University of Missouri researchers state that awareness of mortality and seeking to become part of something larger and more enduring than one self has benefits.[1] Based on this study, I can guarantee[2] that reading this chapters will make you: exercise more, divorce less, smoke only next to the people you really hate, decrease your militaristic attitudes, and increase your altruism and helpfulness. You are welcome. For me, it simply makes buying something unreasonably expensive and that I likely don't need a lot easier. As long as irrationality does not make it in

---

[1] The paper, "When Death is Good for Life: Considering the Positive Trajectories of Terror Management" was published online on April 5, 2012, in *Personality and Social Psychology Review*, a journal of the Society for Personality and Social Psychology (SPSP).

[2] Then again, another paper asserts that studies are likely to reach false conclusions. Read "Why Most Published Research Findings Are False" (John P. A. Ioannidis, PLOS Medicine Journal.)

my obituary, I am good.

In all seriousness, the reason why I've written about this subject is because of lessons I've learned that could be worthwhile sharing with you, my sole reader.

I've made a sincere and difficult effort to avoid being too cheesy, but Italians at times can not help themselves. So, in a few instances I will use cheap philosophy, common places, and obvious considerations. I am sure some of you will not mind, especially if you are comfortable with poor English expressions, and you've always felt most comfortable in 5th grade.

Pictures have been included not to give you a visual idea of any given concept, but rather because it is a lot easier to cut and paste an image than to write. If you have written anything longer than a postcard, I am sure you will understand.

So, this is the story of a journey through some of my own experiences, in the attempt to understand how to best cope with the way this whole affair will end.

CHAPTER TWO

THE FIRST EXPERIENCE

I have no clear recollection of what year it was – it was almost an emotional concussion. I just remember a few distinct images, like someone taking pictures, snapshots, frames

I recall the visit to the hospital – the unusual and unpleasant smell, her face clearly showing the discomfort and the pain.

Then another snapshot at the moment I glanced at my grandmother on her bed, motionless. *The voices of the people in her house, talking about God-knows-what.*

The next image is me alone, leaning on the blue fence outside her garden, crying.

There was the pain in my neck in church. I could not raise my head for hours. *Looking down to ignore what was before me.*

After the service I did not look up either. I could not see anyone's eyes for fear that I would start to cry again. I had nothing to say, just a feeling of uncontainable sadness, the quiet consciousness that I would never see her again.

Years later I wrote:
I remember the taste of the small raspberries
The bright green of the plants and the flowers of the little garden

I recall her taking care of the soil
Pouring the water for the birds

I can still feel her goodnight kisses
Her tasty meals, her care for me

I remember the time spent playing cards
Reading and talking in the warmth of "our" house

I remember the organized mess in the garage hiding secrets and treasures

I remember the suffering and the tears
With my face leaning on the worn blue bars of the fence

My eyes staring at the now lifeless garden
The mind lost in the still second I saw her

Lying in her bed,
For the last time.

Elenora D'angelo in one of her more modest dresses.

You may think my attachment to my grandmother was because of the free meals, the rice puddings, or the money I made playing card games with her. But there was more than that. "Nonna" Nora offered me the safety and comfort of a quiet place. Never bored, I simply loved spending my summers with her, away from the regular dysfunctions of my family.

I had risked my life many times before that day: From "racing" to work with my motorcycle in the mist of Rome's traffic (and please try 90 mph on the Raccordo Anulare before you dismiss this statement) to bungee jumping, from parachuting from perfectly functional airplanes to learning gymnastics at 33 years old and at 200 lbs. Youth never suggested to me that dying was a possibility, nor a concern. I did hear about it – some people passed; but it was never close, never personal.

Until that day. What I learned that day is that when people die, they are no more. I learned how very painful it is when the person has been such a great part of your life.

I was not prepared by anyone to deal with it – not by my parents, not by my teachers, not by my friends. I really had no one who wanted to talk about it for less than $180 an hour.

It was like all of a sudden having in my mouth a dry, chalky, and bitter pill. No one warned me I actually would have to swallow it, nor was I offered a glass of water to help me shove it down my throat.

CHAPTER THREE

IMAGES OF DEATH:
HOW TO BEST SCARE OURSELVES

When I say "images of death," I am not speaking about images of peak L.A. traffic, but rather about the collective images that along the course of our lives we have associated with death.

Another good day in L.A.

While we are raised to avoid thinking about dying,

there has also been a cultural obsession with creating images that associate dying with fear, horror, and terror. Throughout the ages we see manuscripts, stained glass, churches, sculptures and paintings of death and damnation, where skulls and gruesome demons are depicted in vivid detail.

We don't teach our children to understand, much less deal with, this hardest part of life; yet we sure make a point to make it as fearful as possible. How can we therefore be surprised at our difficulty as adults in negotiating death's implications?

Examples abound, especially in a religious context. A brief glance at history books can show how this cultural conditioning has sunk into our subconscious mind from generation to generation, for thousands of years.

Greek mythology offers one of the first examples of this imagery. The Greeks came up with the idea of depicting death as a demon. While the scary sounding name – *Thánatos* – is perfect for the character, at times they used magnificent sculptures to represent him as a cute-looking boy. Even with wings and a menacing sword, he needed more of an edge.

The Greek Angel of Death as he appears on a column
from the ruined Temple of Artemis at Ephesus.

The poet Hesiod made it scarier. He established in
his book, *Theogony*, that Thánatos is the son of Nyx
(Night) and Erebos (Darkness) – the night and the

darkness giving birth to death. *Now we are going somewhere.* The Greeks may not be too good with handling money, but surely they have a vivid imagination.

But few can meet the challenge of the obscure and extravagant imagery of the final book of the New Testament, *The Book of Revelation.*

As with a mime act, this brief outline of a randomly-chosen selection needs no comment.

Seven Seals are opened.

First Seal: A white horse appears, whose crowned rider has a bow with which to conquer. (6:1-2)
Comment: symbolic. The bow is actually a multiple warhead intercontinental ballistic missile. Quite hard to carry on a horse, indeed.

Second Seal: A red horse appears, whose rider is granted a "great sword" to take peace from the earth. (6:3-4)
Comment: symbolic. Another nuke.

Third Seal: A black horse appears, whose rider has "a pair of balances in his hand," where a voice then says, "A measure of wheat for a penny, and three measures of barley for a penny; and [see] thou hurt not the oil and the wine." (6:5-6)
Comment: I don't know what this means, as I am not good at math. What is he asking again? A nickel,

some weed and a drink?

Fourth Seal: A pale horse appears, whose rider is Death, and Hades follows him. Death was granted a fourth part of the earth, to kill with sword, with hunger, with death, and with the beasts of the earth. (6:7-8)

Comment: No comment, just scary.

I could not find the *actual* photo of the apocalypse horseman. (Credit: Wallsave.com)

Fifth Seal: "Under the altar," appeared the souls of martyrs for the "word of God," who cry out for vengeance. They are given white robes and told to rest until the martyrdom of their brothers is completed. (6:9-11)

Comment: I always liked white robes. Makes you feel clean. What is bothersome is that there is no indication on how to be one of those who cry for vengeance and receive one.

Sixth Seal: (6:12-17): There occurs a great earthquake where "the sun becomes black as sackcloth of hair, and the

moon like blood." (6:12)
Comment: Only in California.

The stars of heaven fall to the earth and the sky recedes like a scroll being rolled up. (6:13-14)
Comment: That sounds really unpleasant. There are about 200 billion stars in our galaxy (my approximation of heaven). If they all fall to the earth, we are doomed.

Every mountain and island is moved out of place. (6:14)
Comment: Underestimation. At the very least! After all the stars crashing down!

The people of earth retreat to caves in the mountains. (6:15)
Comment: Safety at last!

The survivors call upon the mountains and the rocks to fall on them, so as to hide them from the "wrath of the Lamb." (6:16)
Comment: Maybe it was not such a great idea. How do we get out again?

Still not quite at the level of a Quentin Tarantino film, but you get the picture. Thank god for the comforts of religion.

Fast forward to 1475 A.D. "The Beast Acheron," (in the figure below) a giant monster holding lost souls in its mouth, depicts a hell of a vision of what could happen after death.

While hellfire makes for great artwork, it also makes for horrible nightmares.

Simon Marmion and The Beast Acheron, in all its tenderness

Paul Gustave Doré was one of the most successful and prolific French artists (engraver, illustrator, and sculptor) of the mid-19th century. His talent could be best demonstrated by the vivid illustration of Dante Alighieri's words from late editions of *La Divina Commedia* (for those of you that speak English is *The Divine Comedy*).

In one of his pieces, Doré offers another version of the fantastic image we all have (in various iterations) of the dark, emotionless, merciless entity we call death.

The Doré's illustration, *Death on a Pale Horse*

In this race for who-can-scare-the-most-people-wins, we find yet another uplifting example in the colored reproduction of Van Eyck's *Last Judgment*, surely one of the most horrendous products of human imagination.

This scene of hell is quite disturbing. I challenge you to find a representation of death as bizarre as this: a skeleton with bat-like wings, displaying a rare flexibility with legs and arms spread wide open over a chaotic mass of screaming bodies. Clearly hallucinogens were readily available at that time.

Van Eyck's *Last Judgment*

Ready for another day at the office.
(Credit to L-WiN)

Scary, eh?! But guess what? *These images are not real.*

They don't exist outside our collective imagination. Death is neither an entity nor a robed skeleton on a flying black horse, holding a menacing sickle.

Even if intellectually we know and understand that these images are fictional, they do leave a mark – a lasting imprint – in our emotional and subconscious matrix. In the back of our mind, in a certain emotional place of our brain[3], we learn to fear death and its consequences.

[3] To be specific, the dorsal anterior cingulated cortex, a part of the brain that deals with both physical pain and social anxiety or distress.

It takes repeated intellectual effort to appreciate how primitively fantastic these representations truly are. Repeat the exercise enough times, and these images will be about as scary as Snow White's "*Grumpy*."

But don't think this is an overnight effort. In fact it might take centuries. It is not something you can achieve by reading a book, or by having a few tweet exchanges with Oprah.

Keep in mind that it took pretty much all your life to *form* this silent and ingrained fear, so it might take years of laughter to bring the idea of a Grim Reaper back to its rightful proportion.

(Credit to RipClint on deviantart.com)

DARIO D'ANGELO

CHAPTER FOUR

WHO DID NOT TEACH THE TEACHERS?

I am opinionated regarding the flaws and limitations of the "modern" educational system. Having lived in Italy – the land of contradiction and dysfunction – for 28 years, this may not come as a surprise.

I do not hold a different opinion of the American system and, even more broadly, that of the industrialized world.

As students, we spend enormous amounts of time in classrooms memorizing information, and learning skills barely applicable to a given job and rarely usable in real life. It's a system that entirely neglects our need to relate to the practical world and the human condition.

Albert Einstein once said: *"Education is what remains after one has forgotten everything he learned in school."*

Let's face it: there is no instruction manual out there, nor any sort of prep school to ready you for life as a young human. No one teaches about how to deal with emotions. How to manage anger? What is its origin? What to do when the hot girl you fell in love with mercilessly dumps you? What it means when she says, "It's not you, it's me"? How to cope with sorrow? Am I good enough? What is death; and more importantly, what is life? How am I related to the environment? Why does Godzilla only attack Japan?[4] Why Italy is always on the verge of collapse? The most important questions of the human experience are swept under the rug or treated on a need-to-know basis like some sort of CIA covert operation.

Many argue that answering these questions is a job for parents, perhaps what parenting is all about. True – but the problem is that since no education is mandated for parents, many end up not knowing exactly what to teach a child and/or simply delegate this responsibility to unqualified others. The questions may seem too hard or uncomfortable to discuss, and our jobs make us too busy or too tired to try.

The point is: there is little meaning in working so hard to send your children to college and trying to make their lives easier than yours, if they are not

---

[4] O.K. smarty-pants, if you really want to be educated, it attacked New York once in 1998.

receiving guidance on how to deal with the most fundamental subjects of the human experience.

So feel free to demand answers from your parents; in the meantime, I will be offering a point of view that I hope is at least entertaining.

The easy one first: Why Italy is always on the verge of collapse? Because of the Italians. *True story.*

CHAPTER FIVE

FOR THOSE WHO WANT TO LIVE FOREVER

Reductio ad absurdum, an expression that the Latins took from the Greeks, is used as argument to demonstrate a statement is false by showing that a false, untenable, or absurd result follows from its acceptance.

Indulge in the following imaginary situation but possibly without falling in a Todd Akin-like delusional state[5].

Let's say you hate death and you think it is absolutely outrageous that we have to deal with it.

Let's also assume that in this universe, you are a

---

[5] Dumb joke based on a dumber individual. Todd Akin was a 2012 Missouri's Republican Senator Candidate who in an interview on national TV was asked a question about allowing abortions in the case of rape. He said, and I quote, "From what I understand from doctors, if it's a legitimate rape, the female body has ways to try to shut that whole thing down." If you ever feel stupid, just remember Todd and you'll be better.

god with limited powers: solely able to decide who/what lives and who/what dies. At first, in your immense graciousness you might decide to grant eternal life to everything from the very beginning of time. Sounds grand, but there are a number of problems. Without dwelling too deeply into scientific details (some of which are in a later chapter), the only way we could now have planets with elements like water, carbon, and oxygen, is because all the early hyper-giant stars died. Not a big deal, you then decide to make only stars die to allow the formation of planetary systems, like the solar system and planets like ours.

So we end up with a planet with biological life; but since nothing dies, species overcrowding occurs and does so quite quickly. At best, the most aggressive and prolific creatures will dominate all else. *Okay, got it. Who cares about them, anyways!* Let's give all creatures only limited life, so we can go through the evolutionary process as we know it, to finally arrive to humanity as it is today.

Everything looks good. It's decided that in this universe only humans will be living forever.

I am sure you start to see the problem. Since humans seem to really like breeding like rabbits in a monastery, in a few thousand years there will be so many people that the ability of the planet to sustain anyone who eats will be non-existent. We will devour anything organic, kill anything that can be eaten, drink everything that can be drank. Not only will we end up with a world looking like south-shore Chicago, but at some point there will be only endless commuting and a lot of nothing for everyone.

Imagine being stuck at 7:00 a.m. in a New York subway train towards Manhattan at rush hour with people as hungry as those in any random Sub-Saharan Africa country for years on end. Sounds like a nightmare to me.

Dramatization - In this image, only a few are hungry

Fine! I got it! This god is getting a little annoyed. For one last try, you decide to let only one person live forever – namely, the actual you.

You get married, you see your wife transform

from Anna Torv into Meryl Streep. Eventually she dies, and that is not fun. Your kids become adults, then – in what feels like a short few years – you have to witness their deaths too. Getting married for the 15th time does not sound too exciting. You've gone around the world 111 times and you've run out of fun things to do, nice places to see, interesting people to meet. Nothing is really new. Reality shows become finally unbearable, but you would do anything not to watch another million sunsets and sunrises.

It is reasonable to imagine that slowly but surely life would become an oppressing, dreadful, inescapable bore – so tragic that you'd wish you could die. Even if your body could live forever, I doubt your mind could too.

If you don't believe me, just read the words of the noble Elf Elrond, Lord of Rivendell. I am not making this up. This is really what he said when his daughter, the beautiful princess Arwen, chose to be with her lover Aragorn, a mortal human. (Elves, as I am sure you know, are an immortal race of middle earth).

"If Sauron[6] is defeated and Aragorn made king and all that you hope for comes true, you will still have to taste the bitterness of mortality.
Whether by the sword or the slow decay of time, Aragorn

---

[6] Long Story. In a nutshell: a huge, mean, powerful and very bad guy.

will die. And there will be no comfort for you. No comfort to ease the pain of his passing. He will come to death, an image of the splendor of the kings of Men, in a glory undimmed before the breaking of the world.

But you… my daughter, you will linger on in darkness and in doubt as nightfall in winter that comes without a star. Here you will dwell, bound to your grief, under the fading trees until the entire world is changed and the long years of your life are utterly spent."[7]

Death is not simply a call of the universe to regenerate itself, but a necessity that enables the evolution towards something greater, and better. It is not an unjust, merciless and inevitable event; but rather the premise for any species to thrive, and for any system to be sustainable.

In many ways, death is the good fortune that allows us to be here talking about this. It's the instrument that teaches us the only way to truly appreciate the uniqueness of an experience so delicate, so impermanent, yet so beautiful.

Two sides of the same coin. The positive and the negative poles of a magnet. Life and death. One needs the other, one part of the other; one cannot exist without the other.

---

[7] If you don't believe me, watch "The Lord of the Rings – The Two Towers" based on J. R. R. Tolkien's manuscripts.

You could say that the thought of ceasing to exist is as painful as living is joyful.

CHAPTER SIX

PRACTICAL METAPHYSICS

From the Tao Te Ching: *We shape clay into a pot, but it is the emptiness inside that holds whatever we want.*

I have always struggled with the idea that philosophy in general, and metaphysics in particular, is entirely an intellectual exercise without any practical, real world, everyday application, akin to some sort of useless theory.

If you are not sleeping by now, what follows will knock you out.

I define metaphysics as the way we choose to see the world. The way we choose to see the world seems to determine the way we feel, and that in turn will likely affect a wide range of human emotions.

The way we choose to relate to events and the principles from which we choose to operate become the basic mechanism behind every action and every decision made in everyday life.

In other words, in one way or the other, everyone operates using certain Metaphysics, but few ask themselves, *Is this the way I want to see the world? Is this what I choose to pour inside the pot?*

I learned to appreciate philosophy because it forced me to seek answers to the deepest and most tormenting questions, those unsettling thoughts that would creep up in my mind when I was alone and not entertained or engaged.

I ultimately concluded that *the answers to these most profound questions* had nothing to do with the abstraction of stoic concepts, and everything to do with reaching a certain understanding of the concrete, material, and physical world. I was able to come to terms with the challenging events of everyday life.

To understand how to deal with death, we must choose the metaphysics that can make us understand life, but rarely do we stop our trivial and habitual thinking to contemplate it.

As Shakespeare wrote: *There is nothing either good or bad but thinking makes it so.*

CHAPTER SEVEN

RISKING IT ALL TO FEEL ALIVE

Thirty nine degrees. Winter just passed, but it is freezing cold. You can still see how many cold nights have passed just by watching the snow atop the sharp stones of ancient ruins and the impervious Corrin's tower[8], the white poorly masking the black rocks of the walls in the peaceful town of Peel.

In this place time can stand still. The brown and green of a frozen soil, the rare quiet of gently flowing hills, and the ancient footpaths, creating the today of a thousand years.

It is rare not to see the thick grey fog on the island; but when spring finally comes, the crisp air of a sunny morning just after sunrise transforms

---

[8] Corrin's Tower is a large square building, 50 feet high. It was erected about sixty years ago by Mr. Thomas Corrin, a somewhat eccentric gentleman, who died at his residence in Knockaloe near the Tower.

unspoiled bleak into absolutely stunning, no matter where you are.

(Credit: doncontrols from Flickr.com)

This is the Isle of Man, also known as Mann, a small island in the middle of everything. Centered in the Irish Sea, it sits almost equidistant between Great Britain and Ireland, and is a tax heaven that politically does not belong to the United Kingdom, or the Commonwealth.

These are 220 square miles of independence and with a people's attitude to show for it, yet never at the expense of a welcoming spirit. They make you feel you are visiting an old friend.

I wish I had gone there at least once.

Mann is a place that can not be famous for much. Few people live there, and with a climate that only the local can describe as temperate, it is not an ideal place for family vacations.

You are probably wondering why this little known island makes it to these pages.

Even if not much happens all year, there is a unique event in the middle of June: *The Isle of Man Tourist Trophy Motorcycle Race.*

The start of the Superbike at Isle of Man TT
(Credit: Stephen Davison/Pacemaker Press International)

Make no mistake: this is no run-of-the-mill motorcycle race. What makes the TT relevant, and winning it unusually valiant, are the 240 people who have died trying. From 1907 to today, it is rare to have a race without a casualty.

Yet, for some reason this has been – and arguably still is - the most prestigious race in the world, and here is where the greatest motorcycle riders of all time were made.

TT's race route on the Isle of Man

Yes, even in today's world where any political decision cannot be made without an obsession for safety, this is the most anachronistic of all professional sporting events. Everyone knows that someone will, with a reasonable statistical certainty, die; yet there is overwhelming determination to keep the race going.

The risk comes from going to high speeds – some sections in excess of 180 mph – on narrow, twisting streets flanked by stone walls, sidewalks, poorly-buffered light poles, and even buildings.

To put things in perspective, a typical 37.7-mile lap is covered in under 18 minutes – *yes, eighteen minutes*. The *average* speed on this course is around 130 mph.

John McGuiness, the man now legend who likely inspired the expressions "Scary Fast" and "Godspeed." (Credit: roadracingsupporters.com / Isle of Man TT)

Who are these 200 men and women participating? Adrenaline freaks? Young, reckless, egocentric? Suicidal single males? Call them what you wish, but the truth is that they are people like me and you, with a notable exception: they dare to define their lives by risking everything. How? With skill, bravery, determination, and a huge set of balls.

Let's explore the stereotypes you might have of these racers.

Young or single? Eeeh, not so... John McGuiness, father of two, was 41 years old when he won the TT in 2012 for the Superbike class. Second place was occupied by Cameron Donald at 36 years old. Third place? Bruce Anstey, born August 21st, 1969.

So is it about egos or money? Not a chance. This is not Grand Prix Racing. The TT Grand Prize is about $48,000, when it may cost around $40,000 to have competitive equipment. For some privateers, this is likely all they have saved.

Fame? Ah-ah! Very few know these racers' names, and even less their faces. Most of them have regular jobs and families to feed. Watch any interview and you will see only individuals with a disarming honesty and unassuming personality. They show the confidence of those who accept their failures, and the modesty of those who do not hold on to their successes.

I know what you are thinking, but I am going to talk about something else. The Isle of Man TT Race is not an example of Sigmund Freud's *"Eros – Thanatos"* theory.[9] Despite Dr Freud's crisp

---

[9] Freud believed that people are driven by two conflicting central desires: the life drive libido or Eros (survival, propagation, hunger, thirst, and sex) and the death drive, also termed "Thanatos".

imagination and entertaining pseudo-scientific theories of the mechanisms behind the human mind (his own), this race is neither a death drive nor an instinct toward self-destruction. Rather, it is the very opposite: It is a drive to live every breath at its fullest, create moments without past or future, and assert the right to pursue your passions at risk, in a risk-averse world.

Once the race is over – just like survivors of a catastrophe, some racers gain a new appreciation for life: *I made it. What a blast. I am alive. I want to do it again!*

In my mind, these guys live *carpe diem* far more than one can by watching reality shows, or by arguing who hurt each other's feelings the most

Let me give you a glimpse of the mindset of this rare breed of racer. Guy Martin, one of the most popular riders who in 2010 crashed his Honda CBR1000RR at over 170mph, hitting a stone wall and destroying his bike in a huge fireball, was asked: *"...[Does] that dice with death affect your approach to the race?"*

"No, of course not," he said. *"Sounds worse than it was...I was injured but it wasn't bad - I broke eight ribs, punctured my lungs and broke my back in a few places - but the worst thing was I had a week in hospital and then another week off work."*

Geez, what a drama queen! His daytime job? Quite important, indeed: he is a mechanic.

William Dunlop lost his father as well as his uncle in racing accidents, but continues to compete alongside his brother Michael at Mann. In an interview, he was asked how the death of his father affected his decision to carry on in a race as dangerous as the Isle of Man TT. This is his answer:

"....It is kind of weird when it is all sorted out... I don't really know how to say it. It is just the way it was... When you are part of it, when you see what they got out of it, you realize how great is to be involved in it... For people who have never been involved in it, they may think you are just throwing your life away. But we are all going to die, and I am not going to worry about it as long as I can enjoy myself."

This is one situation where individuals transcend the idea that the value of life lies within a safe existence. For them, life's purpose is not self-preservation at all costs, or for the sake of itself, but rather an experience to be enjoyed in whatever way that makes them feel alive.

Émile François Zola, one of the most provoking French writers of the mid 1800s, stated:

If you ask me what I came into this life to do, I will tell you: I came to live out loud.

CHAPTER EIGHT

FEAR OF DEATH?
TRY JUMPING OUT OF AN AIRPLANE

I was about 20 years old. I had decided to join the military for a number of reasons, one of which is me being an idiot. Another one, and probably the most important, is that in Italy at that time, I had little choice.

I was interested in finding out what "I" was made of, whatever that was – or even better, what "I" was all about, since before then it was all very confusing.

What happens when "I" feels fear? Can "I" achieve the daring? Can "I" overcome mental abuse? Will "I" feel like shit in the process? To make sure I was going to answer *yes* to all the above, I chose to train as an Army officer for five grueling months.

Ultimately I joined the 3rd Battalion *Poggio Rusco,* 9th Paratroopers Company of the elite division *Folgore.* It was one of the hardest things a young, semi-aware kid could do in the land of mamma, pasta, pizza, and good wine.

Not me, but you get the picture

Generally speaking, in the paratroopers there are three major challenges you have to overcome: mental stress, brutal physical conditioning, and fear a.k.a. *you-will-be-scared-to-death* jumping out of airplanes and helicopters. The latter was surely the more eventful, and the very reason why I am writing this chapter.

This is not a Rambo recollection. I guarantee no minds will be traumatized beyond my own.

It was about 5:00 p.m. and my platoon and I were sitting on the runway next to the cute looking "cow." The "cow" was not actually a cow, but a twin turboprop-engine military airplane G.222, used for tactical transport.

The cow ready to fly... just like the pig

This was the last of the five training jumps I was supposed to perform in order to get the "wings," the ultimate goal of these tough months of training.

The picture was quite nice: Sun was about to set in the charming Tuscan airport of Pisa, with the smell of combusted jet fuel from the G.222 turbines burning my nostrils and tearing up my eyes; My comrades seemingly too preoccupied to make fun of any expression I may have had; The parachute-packing looking more or less acceptable. All good!

Fifteen minutes before loading, I was checking

the piece of paper in the pocket of the parachute backpack for the name of the dude who folded and packed my controlled-descent device. Suddenly, I had a paralyzing fear, a terrifying feeling that this was going to be my last jump. It felt like the day I was going die.

Ready to "go" so to speak
(Credit: Fabio Vitali on Flickr.com)

I did go to the bathroom a few hours before, but even so, at that point my options to have a time-out were very limited. Screaming like a little girl as the jumpmaster tries to "nudge" me outside the airplane was not one of them. I'd rather have my remains unevenly distributed on 40 square feet of the landing zone than suffer that level of humiliation.

Option number two? Not to board the airplane. You are allowed to do that, granted that you will get kicked out of the paratroopers and spend the rest of your military life as a rational human being. That was an unacceptable implication, as it would have shattered all my dreams to become the Maverick in *Top Gun*. So, no way; definitely not an option.

My third possibility was to overcome this fear. I did not know how though. So I started thinking: *Ok, let's say I am right, and I will die. Well... it should not be too painful as I would "land" at terminal velocity[10]. Maybe a moment or two... but I doubt anything more. So now I am dead, and... what? Nothing. I am dead. Good! Not much to lose then.*

I boarded the airplane with the confidence of a veteran. A smirk on my face reflected the brashness of someone who knew what was next and how to handle it. In that moment, the certainty that I was going to die liberated me COMPLETELY of all my fears. I was actually kind of happy to have come this far. This was the best I could do, and all in all, I had a fun life. Even more comforting was the idea that I was going out with a bang (or a splat if you prefer), rather than a slow and painful fading.

On the airplane, I was first in line at the door, ready to jump with my right foot partially outside the fuselage, the turboprop wind on my face, still smelling the darn jet fuel (airplane design at its best),

---

[10] Based on wind resistance, the terminal velocity of a skydiver in a belly-to-earth (i.e. face down) free-fall position is about 195 km/h (122 mph or 54 m/s). Not as interesting as much as it is scary. Try it.

and looking 700 ft down to the little houses passing by. No fear, just the thrill of the last few moments. I could not wait to jump, and so I did with abandon and some degree of joy.

Looks like fun, eh!?!
(credit to defense.gov)

Well, I was wrong – I did not die, as you probably guessed, but...

As I was gently gliding towards the ground, the silence felt implausibly enjoyable. The breeze felt like a crib. All was peaceful and at the same time exhilarating. This was just before noticing I was about to collide with a fellow paratrooper. A routine jump suddenly transformed into a brief, one-way field trip into the unknown.

For those who do not know, a collision on a static line launch is a bit tricky. Because these jumps are at very low altitude, if something bad happens you have about 15 seconds to figure out that your emergency parachute is useless and how in the world you are going to get out of the disaster.

To make the short story shorter, I spent my 15 seconds trying to *get off of* my comrade's parachute. While I was quite comfortable laying into it (imagine a gigantic, silky, and super soft air mattress), I realized that having the chute below siphon the air that was to keep *my* parachute open could be a small issue.

Indeed, that was the case.

I plunged to the ground for what felt a million miles, while reaching for the emergency parachute's handle, ready to pull it. Of course, at less than 100 feet from the ground, it is more a psychological victory (e.g. "I paid attention to the instructor!") than a way to save your life. The emergency chute takes quite some time to open, and if your main chute is open at the same time, all you can hope to achieve is a tangle of the two. So I smiled and hoped that the primary one would at some point reopen.

It did. But something else happened.

While I admit the landing was not very pretty,

once I stood up I realized that I survived. *I was alive and in one piece.* As I took my helmet off and wiped my sweat, I felt ecstatic and laughed my heart out. I considered breathing the warm evening air of the Tuscan Altopascio fields a truly incredible miracle.

It is difficult to overstate the exhilaration I had at that very moment; especially after seeing the ambulance come at full speed, (I assume) to recover what could have been left of our bodies.

So what did I learn from this experience?

A couple of things: First, jumping off airplanes can be kind of dangerous. The second lesson is the parallel between this encounter and our daily experience living life. I discovered the awe of *being* that lies within the complete, sincere, and profound acceptance that I *may not be.* This is a place from which we can accept the inevitable, and face our own mortality with a sense of peace.

Thus, I uncovered what for me is the great irony of the universe: *Without the prospect of death, we would not be able to experience fully the awe of being alive.*

I guess this is where I should say "thank you."

From William Shakespeare's play *Julius Caesar.* Act II, Scene II:

Cowards die many times before their deaths; The valiant never taste of death but once.

Of all the wonders that I yet have heard, it seems to me most strange that men should fear; Seeing that death, a necessary end, will come when it will come.

DARIO D'ANGELO

CHAPTER NINE

THE SECOND EXPERIENCE

This story has a happy ending so no need for tissues.

Nathera's diagnosis was Non-Hodgkin's Lymphoma. Lymphoma is a term for cancers that develop from the cells of the lymphatic system (part of the body's immune system) called lymphocytes. Lymphocytes are a subset of white blood cells responsible for immunity and fighting infections. Lymphomas first start from errors that occur in the DNA of lymphocytes in either the lymph nodes or other lymphoid tissue. When one of these cells undergoes a transformation into a malignant cell and begins to grow abnormally, lymphoma arises.

It was sometime in September 2011 when complications most likely from the second round of chemotherapy forced Nathera to be hospitalized.

Her condition deteriorated very rapidly, and after just the third day at the hospital it looked like life was sucked away from her. The possibility of death marked everyone's mind.

The attitude I try to have in these circumstances is dignity and non-drama. If someone is dying, try to remove your self-pity from the picture. This is not something you can necessarily impose on yourself, but you try to project that level of conviction.

Several sleepless nights followed in those days. Nathera is my wife Tina's mother.

As we were laying in bed, Tina was desperately trying to make sense of it all. *The fear of coexisting with an irreversible loss. The torturing thoughts of regret. Wondering about the many places and the many things that would have reminded her of her mom.*

Those nights inspired this book, as I was trying to offer my wife – and probably myself – a perspective that could be somewhat comforting. A way to somehow deal with "it." The essence of those conversations is what you have been reading in these pages.

Nathera ended up being healthier than even I, but from this experience I learned another couple of things. One is that even if cancer is not fun, going to the hospital to get treated is worse.

The other realization is that there is a clear

distinction to be made when someone very close to you is in serious risk of passing: The concern you have for them dying as opposed to your own feelings of loss (the *"What will happen to me?"*).

So let's explore the two aspects separately since they are... well, separate.

The person dying is usually quite at peace with the idea. Or at least Nathera seemed to be. As was I in my own experience with the parachuting incident. Once you feel something is dramatically wrong and realize the chance of not making it is a clear and present danger, there is often a certain sense of acceptance, the *"It was a good run"* attitude.

That leaves us with "What will happen to me?" For that, you have to read the next chapters. Press on.

CHAPTER TEN

POPPING OUT OF EXISTENCE: WHAT HAPPENS NEXT?

Well, hard to say – not just for me, but also for those who are not dead yet, and sadly even for those who are dead.

I hate to break it to you, but neither Popes (the emeritus and the regular one), arguably the closest thing to superheroes we have, know for a fact. Yes, you heard me; the leader of the worldwide Catholic Church, the successor of the fisherman formally known as Saint Peter, the infallible and the revered voice(s) of God, the owner of fancy robes, big hats, and red pretty shoes… does not know for sure. He has faith that he got it right… but so do I.

So let's assume we are logical entities for a moment. While we clearly can not know what happens next, and no one on the other side can really tweet about it, let's try first to guess what death is really NOT.

It is not like being buried alive, as – clearly – there is no one alive. It is not like a deep slumber, as there is no one who is *that* tired. It is not like being in the dark forever, as there is no one to "be" in the dark. It is not eternal boredom. You are not going to regret not being alive, because there's no one to regret it. It's hard to see the problem from the dead person's point of view.

Imagine how you felt before you were born. My assumption is that it would "feel" the same. And if it's going to feel just like before you were born, that ain't too bad. From your perspective, besides this blink we call life, there was never really anything – not you nor everything else.

Personally, I do not care much for that nearly eternal part of my pre-life. But it does help me to presume that my post-life will be as uneventful as my pre-life. That allows me to say with outward confidence, when my loved ones fear for my safety: *No worries. If it happens, I know where I'm going.*

A Zen Master once suggested that while we live, we should enjoy the mystery and the beauty of life rather than worry about what comes after life. Live today without worrying about tomorrow, for tomorrow will have its own worries.

CHAPTER ELEVEN

THE SECRET OF ACCEPTANCE

Despite my devilish good looks that for some reason only my mom mentioned, I got married quite late in life. I like to think I waited for the right person, even if I suspected that the right person wasn't looking that hard, or worse, was a figment of my imagination.

In the end what really supported my choice was Barak Obama. Yes, the president of the US of A. Technically it was not really him in person, but one of his interviews. If you are as curious as I, you will have no choice but read on to end of the chapter to find out how.

My way of justifying uncountable romantic failures and unmentionable sins was that at least when I got married I would have tried everything; more importantly, that once married, I would know that there was nothing I was missing out on. I would be in a relationship with no doubts, knowing that anything other than what I have did not, cannot and would not work out.

It was a choice with no regrets. Yeah, sure! Pretty words, but nothing is that easy. The not-so-romantic truth is that my not-so-soon-to-be wife rejected me FOUR times before considering having a stable relationship.

My instincts were telling me she was the right person while she was telling me I was better off trying to go find the right person.

I had to take a chance and risk a broken heart – four times, that is; and each time more painful than the previous, to the point that I had about 1/16th of a heart left for purposes other than beating.

It took a great deal of good old fashioned denial and an unexplainable refusal to acknowledge what seemed the unavoidable reality of the situation. I was unable to do what all my friends – and probably some of my most merciful enemies – suggested: forget about her, and go fishing.

A good plan, sure. But there were two problems with it. First, I hate fishing. Secondly, it is quite hard to forget someone who lives in the same condo complex and who for some evil reason keeps calling you at the very moment you are about to move on. The third problem, which I am sure you did not see coming, was that I really had fun when I was with her. Fortunately for me, I have an incredibly hard time giving up fun under all circumstances.

The ultimate prize for the frame of mind that guided me was discovering a life far better than what I could have ever hoped for.

How is this relevant to our subject? I found that there could be an analogy between this experience and the way life can be approached.

Are we able do what feels right despite what some think is wrong? In this example, I was able to. But what is more important was the liberating realization that there is really no "right choice" or "wrong choice," but just a path. The refreshing benefit of walking on this path is that often times it leaves you with no regrets. All you really need is the awareness of why you are doing it and the consciousness that you did the best you could under the circumstances. *Easy.*

An analogy that can help articulate this concept is the path of a water stream on a slope. When water flows, it simply follows its nature – to flow – and is guided by the nature of its environment – the soil, the stones and everything around it.

When the stream hits a rock, it does what its nature and its environment suggests. It goes around the rock, to the left or to the right. Is one direction the right direction? Hardly. Either direction is simply part of the water's path. Is the water's hitting the rock a sign of a failure to go in a straight line? Is it an undesired destination? No, not really. The rock is just part of the path, a part of the environment, and without any particular meaning. The water will flow around the rock because that is what it is to be water, rock, and soil.

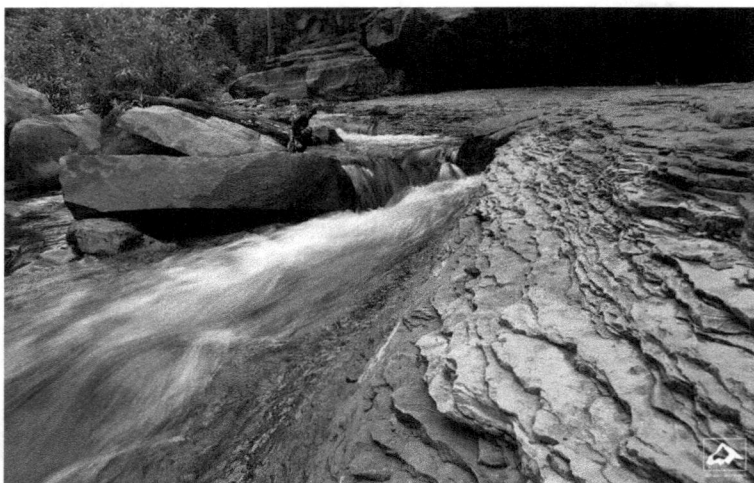

(Credit to Isaac Borrego from flickr.com)

In my case, I could have considered being dumped the first time a failure and given up on this woman. Instead I tried to give no meaning to the event. Just like the stream hitting a rock, I just chose to simply flow to one side and see what would happen next. With just a few days of deep and torturing disappointment, and a short-lived self-pity, I was able to move on without any additional drama or resentment.

The second, third and fourth break up are a lot more difficult to justify, but we will get to that later.

Are we able to take the opportunity to experience, even if it might be risky? Past lessons made me recognize that a life void of risks holds little interest, virtually no possibilities, and certainly no joy. If you stop to think about it, the very nature of something that is truly fun, exciting or exhilarating often times resides in calculated risk-taking.

Are we able to empty the events of drama? Maybe we cannot completely, but it is surely important not to have too much of it either. Most of what tends to emotionally upset us is pondering the inconsequential. While there is indeed a weird comfort in diving into self-pity and dwelling on our emotions, it is an exercise that often becomes pointlessly painful and mildly depressing.

Some believe that is how you fill your life, but look closely and you will discover only thoughts without positive consequences and of no substance.

I believe the best cure when feeling sad is to take care of anything that is not self. It is an unusual, yet effective way to be selfish. When you give time, effort, and energy toward doing good to others – people or animals – you feel undeniably good about it. It is surprising how much serving others can lift your moods, and lighten your spirit.

Martin Luther King Jr. said:

Those who are not looking for happiness are the most likely to find it, because those who are searching forget that the surest way to be happy is to seek happiness for others.

Are we able to recognize that there are only a few events that are truly serious? There is underrated power in a proper perspective on events, dislikes, arguments, litigiousness, and doubts. Once you appreciate the great scheme of things – what *really* matters – and you compare it to what you are dealing with, most choices become simple, and decisions a lot easier to make. On the other hand, if you're serious enough then anything is a problem.

Are we able to pursue those actions that make us smile, or makes us happy? I find it less complicated to set aside my doubts and uncertainties and shift my focus to what gives me mindless happiness.

Indeed, I am convinced that as a country we should all work hard on doing things that make us happy, and measure our wealth not by the dollars made, or by the size of economy, but by the gaiety of our people. Working to accumulate money seems pure silliness to me, as much as measuring the health of our society by our GDP[11]. I'd rather spend my

---

[11] The gross domestic product (GDP) is one the primary indicators used to gauge the health of a country's economy. It represents the total dollar value of all goods/services produced over a specific time period.

energy finding ways to chase play, to choose experience, to pursue what makes me feel my heart beat even for just a moment, to seek what brings the shine of excitement in our eyes. There, I know, is where *a life with no regrets* ultimately lies.

My final thoughts on this subject fall inevitably on the last of all evils in Pandora 's Box[12]: the spirit of Hope. The fact that Hope is the *last* of the evils in the box might sound counterintuitive, but when taken literally, it is actually very profound. In this case, I mean the "hope" that the future holds – something better or something more than what the present does.

Nothing expresses this better than the words of Alan Watts, one of the most brilliant philosophers of my lifetime, in one of his lectures:

[... we say...] I've arrived. But I feel slightly cheated because I feel just the same as I always felt. Something is missing. I have no longer a future.

This policy will enable you to retire in comfort at sixty five, and you will be able to look forward to that. And you are

---

[12]In classical Greek mythology, Pandora was the first woman on Earth. After her creation Zeus gave Pandora a beautiful container – with instructions not to open it under any circumstance. Compelled by her curiosity (given to her by the gods), Pandora opened it, and all evil contained therein escaped and spread over the earth. She hastened to close the container, but the whole contents had escaped, except for one thing that lay at the bottom – the Spirit of Hope named Elpis.

delighted. And you buy the policy and at sixty five you retire thinking that this is the attainment of the goal of life, except that you have prostate trouble, false teeth and wrinkled skin. And you are a materialist. You are a phantom, you are an abstractionist, you are just nowhere, because you never were told, and never realized that eternity is now.

It is the same as time, it is an abstraction. It is a convenience so that I can arrange to meet you at the corner of Main and I, or whatever it is, at 4 o'clock. Great. But let us not be fooled by it. It is not real. So people who do not live in the present, have absolutely no use for making plans. Because you see ordinary people who believe in time, and who believe that they are living for their future, they make plenty of plans. Yeah. But when the plans mature, and they come off, the people are not there to enjoy them. They are planning something else. And they are like donkeys perpetually running after carrots that are attached to their own collars. And so they are never here, they never get there, they are never alive, they are perpetually frustrated, and therefore they are always thinking. "Someday it is going to happen." And because it never does, they want more time, more time please, more time. They are terrified of death because death stops the future. And so you never got there. You never have it. There is always, somewhere around the corner.

Is this the secret to the acceptance of the inevitable? Only you can answer that.

That's why it's a secret.

For me, in order to be ready to die on the spot and be absolutely ok with it, I have to be in a position to say: *I've lived a full life, and even if I am not sure I want to go anywhere, I know I tried my best to make it as fun, enjoyable and worthy as it could have been.*

If you are still wondering why I said that a Barack Obama interview was what really supported my choice to pursue my wife's attentions and withstand four break-ups, this is the answer.

A few days after the second break up, I heard an interview of the President in which he was describing how he ended up marrying Michelle. She had declined his invitation for a date four times. I said *"Four times??* How in the world can you continue to pursue someone who rejects you four times?? How do you find the conviction that you are pursuing the woman and not harassing her?" But then I thought, *He must have known that it was the right choice, since now they seem really happy and in love.*

Suddenly, it occurred to me. All my previous relationships started as great, exciting, and fun experiences, and yet they inexorably ended with struggle, some sadness and a temporary misery. This story was clearly different, with a start as miserable and difficult as you could fashion. Just by reverse logic it must mean that the end was destined to be great. So when she broke up with me the third time, I KNEW I was onto something really special.

CHAPTER TWELVE

WHAT ABOUT ME?
NO WORRIES, YOU'LL CATCH-UP
IN NO TIME

I hope by now it is clear that for me, the hardest thing to negotiate is not the idea of the "I" dying; we can find ways to accept it, to prepare for it, and live with the idea of it. The loss of someone close is quite a different deal.

I keep thinking about parents I know who lost their 15-year-old son to an incurable disease some time ago – *how would they react reading this Chapter?*

The challenge is to say something that not only would be of meaning, but that would also resemble a consolation to such a profound loss; it feels as easy and as important as going to get two ice cubes from the top of Mount Everest.

Not as hard as it looks… when you aren't the one doing the climb.
(Credit: Fedor Filippovich Konyukhov.
Web: konyukhov.ru)

There are not too many ways to make sense of it, but I will attempt the climb anyway, and see if I can bring back at least one ice cube.

Nobody is trying to be cute here, so let me state clearly: the anguish and grief that immediately follows the weeks and months after someone's passing transcends any intellectual understanding or rationalization. It is raw and radical.

It is surmountable and bearable only by time going by. There are no words, no books or no concepts that will make anyone feel better in that time span. It is what it is, and has to be accepted as the inevitable consequence of an inevitable event.

Just like when you are slapped in the face and your cheek burns, you just have to bear the pain and wait for it to go away.

After that, you try to deal with the reality of what comes next.

A part of us irrationally feels bad for the person who is gone. But feelings as such are as understandable as they are unfounded. It is like worrying that someone is hungry when he/she is not hungry.

The person went back to where he/she came from, to the eternal energy source that is everything we know, and all of we do not know. He/she is not suffering any longer, and that is no small thing.

Think of the person in the same state he/she was before he/she was born, because it is *exactly* how it is.

Yes of course the person could have lived longer, experienced more – but at least he/she had experienced *more* than nothing. That is positively better than non-being.

If what I stated makes sense, *that leaves us, those "left behind."*

Assuming this is the problem, I offer two points

of view. The first one is: *Beware, time flies.* If you don't believe me and you are older than 30, look in the mirror.

If my case is of any help to describe it: I feel like I was 30 years-old yesterday. To make things worse, it feels like years are passing at an accelerating pace; the older I get, the faster they go. *Grand.* They also seem to accelerate even more when I spend time watching basketball games with losing NBA teams, or writing books no one will read.

Regardless, when eternity is the term of comparison, years seems an implausibly funny length of time to be genuinely concerned about.

So, no worries; you will catch up with those who have passed in no time. From their perspective, you will join them in less than a blink of an eye; and from yours, it will be in two blinks, a few shots of tequila, a couple of kids, a stroll in the park, but not much more. My suggestion to you is: *Enjoy the ride while you can.*

A Zen parable perhaps expresses this with more intellectual elegance:

A man walking across a field encounters a tiger. He fled, the tiger chasing after him. Coming to a cliff, he caught hold of a wild vine and swung himself over the edge. The tiger sniffed at him from above. Terrified, the man looked down to where, far below, another tiger had come, waiting to eat him. Two mice, one white and one black, little by little began to gnaw away at the vine. The man saw a luscious strawberry near him. Grasping the vine in one hand, he plucked the strawberry with the other. How sweet it tasted!

The other somewhat comforting idea – and I hope not too cheesy – is that everyone leaves a mark on everything touched, not only in material objects given, taken or broken, but also on our experiences.

When we interact with someone, when we love, when lives intertwine, we create a new reality in which neither party is the way he/she was before the interaction.

The experiences we share are like the rowing strokes of an oar in a placid lake. Each stroke gently pushes the vessel in a direction. You might not feel it at the same moment, but by virtue of that very interaction, you moved; you are in a place other then the one you were. In a very concrete and non-spiritual way, the people we are close to never leave our lives because they become part of who we are now. They cannot be lost and they are hardly far, because they are part of a new version of us and changed our course unarguably and permanently.

We are where we are – and more importantly *who we are* – because of the changes their presence brought to our lives.

Going places with our dear ones.
(Credit: P.U.N.K from Flickr.com)

From the famous BBC show, Blackadder Goes Forth:

Row, row, row your punt,
Gently down the stream.
Belt off, trousers down,
Isn't life a scream?

CHAPTER THIRTEEN

ALL THIS CANNOT BE SERIOUS, SO LET'S PLAY!

I do not mean to cheer you up, but some 4.5 billion years from now the sun will become what is called a "red giant" and cook the earth to a crisp. The red giant will dim, shrink and eventually be barely visible from any point outside the solar system. All we have witnessed will slowly fade into darkness.

This begs the question: what is a point of a planet if it will inexorably and utterly be barbequed? What is the point of a star if its light will be shut off? What is the point of the universe if all will end?

My answer is that the universe and its birth/creation must be something akin to a game, without practical outcome or objective, and for that very reason, non-serious.

What is more interesting is to notice that this quality of "non-seriousness" resonates in almost

73

everything we enjoy doing. It seems that we love life the most when we act without purpose!

What is the purpose of playing a Chopin piano Nocturne? It is surely not to reach the end as fast as possible. Why would anyone listen to a Britney Spears' song? I am certain someone has the answer for that. What is the productivity in playing a baseball game? When you dance, is your goal to arrive at a given point of the dance floor? I hope not, since this would be an inefficient way to travel small distances. We do these things because they are fun.

If you ask people what they truly enjoy, cherish, or savor, chances are they would describe something without a real practical purpose – something senseless, relatively unproductive, and likely hard to explain. To reword a quote from Niccolo Machiavelli, a philosopher of the 1500s: *The end does **not** justify the means.*

How liberating. Finally, and at last, I can be proud of being useless and even have a good reason to be so.

I, along with a few million other Italians, *love* motor racing. If you think about it, you realize that racing is a sport that has really no point. You go around the track and you finish exactly where you started. There's no practical outcome, no lives saved, and no one will benefit from you arriving first or last.

The objective of it – its only purpose – is having cars go as fast as possible to see who gets there first. Quite childish, yet the most enjoyable entertainment I can think of.

Sports like football, soccer, volleyball, or basketball follow the same footprint. We take a simple object of a somewhat round shape, create a set of arbitrary rules, form two teams, and pit them against each other. While the point is winning the game, in reality there is no tangible or practical outcome if you do win, and conversely there is no punishment for losing. Once the game is over, nothing is left to speak of it other than a day or two of banter. We love sports precisely because they have no purpose, because they are games.

Intriguingly, the only way to play the game well is to have fun in doing it. You will hear countless times a coach telling his players, "Play hard, but have fun with it." Enjoying the game becomes the best way to play and be truly successful at it.

Case in point. LeBron James, one of the greatest basketball players we have today, and arguably a future Hall of Famer, said in an interview with ESPN's Rachel Nichols:

I got to this point by playing this game a certain way, (I'm) getting back to loving the game and having fun with the game... [..] I play the game fun, joyful, and I let my game do all of the talking and I got away from that. That's what I lost last year.

Looks like someone is about to have fun.
(Credit: Mark J. Terrill/Associated Press, and the N.B.A.)

But this is not what I, and many like me, were taught. Many of us go through life without a real appreciation of what we experience. We are raised to go to school and study hard. We are indoctrinated to find a stable job as soon as possible and to work harder. We are compelled to get married and have kids as a social priority. We feel we must sacrifice for the next generation (which in turn will sacrifice for the next, which in turn will make this whole thing a bit bizarre). Then, at last, after working until old age, we search for meaning.

We do not think of life as play, but rather as a

mission with a purpose. We are raised to be goal-oriented and thus develop a compulsion to achieve whatever goal has been set for us. So it all becomes serious because we must be successful. But this is success as defined by others, and often it comes at a cost. We work long hours and really hard as time slips by and happiness evades us. We feel we must go on, but we do not really know why.

Then one day if some of us discover we are just ordinary, and in the shadows of what we believe is failure, we might develop a certain sense of inadequacy. We ask ourselves if we've lived up to this silent expectation: *Am I good enough?*

I am no expert, but this does not sound like a good overall plan.

Step outside the human domain and you will see that everything is simpler. Nature has no need of subjecting itself to this mental pressure. A beautiful willow tree fulfills its potential by its very existence. No one would say: *"Oh, if it only had two more branches," "I was hoping it had 100 or less leaves,"* or *"Too bad this tree is not as tall as the other one."* When a cat grows up it does not need to be a "better cat," a "successful cat," or an "important cat." It is always adequate to the reality and the circumstances it is in. If a cat should have any goal it is to sleep more and murder innocent bunnies less. *You know whom I am talking about, you bad kitty!*

Can aliveness be simply a game, the goal of which is enjoying playing? And as any player of a game, are we always good enough the way we are? Can it be that what we are here for is to grow, appreciate and cherish? Working to build what we believe in rather than to accumulate money? These answers could be the key to the vault of our most profound doubts.

I am not suggesting that your goal in life should be to become a slob. By "play," I do not mean sit on the couch, eat potato chips, and shoot your way up to level 20 of "World of Warcraft" all day until you become as fat as the perfect online multi-player. (Even if you could see it as an ideal vocational career, it will eventually cost more in medications than the online fees you paid.) Of course I am not speaking by personal experience.

The Game has to be played with respect, and with a passion that reflects the dignity of being human. Its rules are not there to limit you, but to define and direct your inherent potential.

The very contradictory and somehow ironic side of this social construct is that some of us do not quite grasp the *meaning of life,* but yet they hang on to life at all costs.

So I leave you with this question: *If life is really the enjoyment of the experience, is there a point in which the game is not worth the candle[13]?*

From the Hamlet Act III, Scene I:

To be, or not to be: that is the question.

---

[13] The expression "is not worth the candle" dates from medieval times, when any nighttime activity had to be lit by candles, an expensive luxury. So when an activity was "not worth the candle," it meant that it wasn't worth the cost of supplying the light.

DARIO D'ANGELO

CHAPTER FOURTEEN

THE EYES OF THE UNIVERSE

If you really want to be scientific about it, each one of us is a manifestation of the universe. I do not mean in an abstract or spiritual way; I mean *literally*.

I will attempt an explanation, but chances are I will lose your attention after the word "scientific." Nevertheless, it is hard to make a point without a logical foundation, unless you are a Tea Party Republican (and if you are, you can safely skip this chapter since I know you think "science" is not a word).

Modern scientific theories strongly suggest that the Universe was born after an event with a deeply inappropriate name[14] of "The Big Bang" aka T_0.

A few moments after T_0 the enormous energy

---

[14] When there are no terms of comparison (e.g. nothing existed) there is technically nothing that can be big.

available started to form particles like electrons, protons, neutrons, and the like. Then atoms came into existence, which created the first, most fundamental, and arguably the most important element of all: hydrogen. The simplest and most widespread element became the first building block from which everything else was formed.

It was hydrogen that eventually cooled down in the form of giant molecular clouds. Gravity played its first trick: gas started to clump and form something odd at that time – stars.

Hydrogen Gas Pillars in the Eagle Nebula (M16)
a Star-Forming Region.
(Credit: NASA, ESA, STScI, J. Hester and P. Scowen
from Arizona State University)

So the first Hypergiant stars were born, but more importantly started dying shortly thereafter in gigantic explosions. This is a clear case in which a death has a role that is as important as life, especially to a living organism.

The Crab Nebula is a supernova remnant, all that remains of a tremendous stellar explosion. Observers in China and Japan recorded the supernova nearly 1,000 years ago in 1054. (Credit: NASA, ESA, J. Hester and A. Loll from Arizona State University)

To explain: as a star burns its fuel by nuclear fusion, it creates heavier and heavier elements. At the end of its life, when the star explodes in a process called *supernova nucleosynthesis,* those elements get dispersed in space and eventually, in a case of perfect recycling, become part of newborn stars.

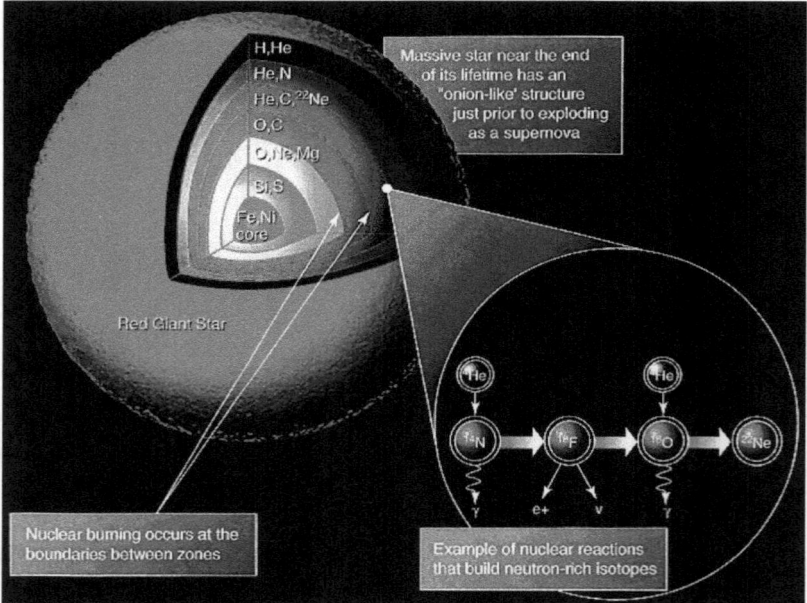

When words are confusing, a picture is a thousand words.

Are you begging to know why this is relevant to you? *Stellar nucleosynthesis* is also known as "you are made out of it." The heavier elements created by the nuclear fusion of hydrogen end up pretty much everywhere in a sequence more or less like this:

Hydrogen -> Helium -> **Carbon** -> Neon -> **Oxygen** -> Silicon -> **Iron.**

Eventually, planets will form from this stuff, and I

hope we all know what grows out a planet made of water and rocks.

Hydrogen, Oxygen, Carbon. Notice anything?! Ninety-three percent of the mass of the human body is made up of just these three elements. We are, <u>literally</u>, made out of stardust.

Why this excruciating explanation? To make the point that this complex, violent, beautiful, nearly eternal universe is expressing itself in the form of galaxies, stars, planets, rocks, water, vegetables, animals, humans, and yes, at last, you. It's a statistical anomaly that is the culmination of countless cycles of life and death of everything that ever happened in the last 13.7 billion years. Congratulations!

Like a cherry tree that uses sunshine, dirt and water to make cherries, an expression of the cherry tree, so the universe uses sunshine, dirt and water to make humans, who are undeniably an expression of the universe.

There are many other expressions of it of course. But humans (some of them at least) have a unique ability in the whole solar system: to be aware of it all.

Sometimes, with the help of alcoholic beverages, paint fumes, and small amounts of illegal substances, I look at the uncountable multitude of stars and galaxies in the night sky and feel that I am part of it all. In those brief moments of lucidity I am the eyes with which the whole shebang is looking back at itself.

If you are not satisfied with the resolution power of your eyes, take a look at the striking images of the Hubble Space Telescope.

One of my favorites is a picture from the Ultra Deep Field collection that captures a very small region of space in the constellation of Fornax. Looking back approximately 13 billion years – shortly after the Big Bang – you can count (or take my word for it) about 10,000 galaxies. Each galaxy has about 200 billion stars like our sun.

(Credit: NASA, ESA, S. Beckwith and the HUDF Team)

If nothing I wrote above made any sense, don't worry. Remember Woody Allen's words:

I'm astounded by people who want to "know" the universe when it's hard enough to find your way around Chinatown.

DARIO D'ANGELO

CHAPTER FIFTEEN

THIRD EXPERIENCE:
WHAT HAPPENS TO THE WORLD
WHEN YOU DIE

I met Trung in early 2000. He was an intern working for my company, IBM, while finishing his degree in Computer Science at the University of California at Berkeley.

We quickly became very good friends despite our eleven year age difference and the cultural gap. Me, Italian, fresh-off-the-boat; and he, not so fresh-off-the-boat, from Saigon. He was probably one of the most generous and giving people I had the honor of calling a friend. His unselfish attitude towards his seemingly thousands of friends was an inspiration. He was always ready to take his shirt off his back and give it you... and I mean literally, as he did not like to wear shirts.

We shared not only interests and passions, but also our lives seem to follow somewhat comparable lines. He was facing the same decisions, similar situations, and comparable romantic dilemmas of single life that I experienced years past.

Trung and I spent a lot of time together working at the same company, thinking about the same things, and pursuing the same interest after work. It was great fun to have finally found a playmate, so far from home. I loved helping out at his dad's shop, arguing about motorcycle racers, or modifying cars with the stubborn conviction we could make things work better. Whether we succeeded was never certain, until the first engine blew up.

Our friendship was without traditional boundaries. I lent him $5,000 – on the spot, no questions asked – to help him buy his first high-performance car. He drove 2,500 miles with me in two days from Houston, TX to San Jose, CA to pick up my first "super car." He was with me the first time I went on a racetrack. We rode motorcycles together many times, and I made him crash twice too many (and was banned from riding with him for two years). We even bought together what we considered "the most good-looking motorcycle ever made," a Ducati 916. Our conversations affected pretty much every aspect of my life to the point I wanted to get a tattoo inspired by of one the things he taught me: *Stop chasing the dragon, catch the dragon.*

Looking back, it's easy to see how at some point

our lives were so intertwined that we could not tell who was who. That is probably why we spontaneously started to call each other *"brothers from different mothers."*

Things eventually changed. Trung quit IBM and started working full-time at his parents' business. Our parallel lives eventually diverged enough that we did not see each other as much. I did not make it mean anything. This is how life works as we negotiate the motions of constant change.

We saw each other every now and then. For the most part when I tried to call, the answers to my "Where are you?" questions were always quite entertaining: *I am in Vegas. I am at my cousin's wedding. I am at my cousin's wedding. I am at my cousin's wedding. I am in Texas. I am at Hooters. I am at my cousin's wedding. I am at a racetrack in Sonoma. I am in Reno.*

The guy did not take the statement *carpe diem* seriously; it was more like *carpe horas*.[15]

And so we begin to drift away.

But I was hurt the day I found out that he became a father of a baby girl and did not let me know. Maybe the fact that he was not married and the

---

[15] Carpe Diem is a Latin expression that literally translated means, "Seize the day". *Carpe Horas* is made up by me and it is used loosely here to mean, "Seize the hour".

relationship with his girlfriend was less than ideal made him feel uneasy. But still… I could not quite accept the fact that he did not share the news with me. I can understand that the disapproval of his parents may have had some influence; nevertheless he should have known that I would have never, ever judged him. The love for my brother was and always will be unconditional.

Just being comical, as always.

On April 17th 2012, my wife told me she saw a Facebook group post with the title, *In Loving Memory of Trung.* These days, this is how you get bad news, it seems. I was going to beat the crap out of him for architecting such a stupid practical joke. *Not funny*, I said.

I called Trung's cell phone a couple of times, but he did not pick up. That was not unusual because the guy was never in the same state for more than few days, and there are about 600,000 Vietnamese in San Jose, CA named Trung. *It could easily be a mistake.* Eventually the truth started to stare at me, and I did not like it. My younger brother Trung was gone, forever.

I will spare you all the details of days, weeks and then months of a bottomless grief, but I will share what I learned from his untimely and tragic death.

Thanks to our particular situation in which our lives were so close for so long that we could very well have been the same person, I got the answer to the apparently unanswerable question: *what will happen to the world after I will die?*

I used to think that when you are dead, you are dead. Everyone's life moves on. The thoughts of you become the past, and eventually, as far as anyone is concerned, you never existed. Basically it's a wash: *Thank you, it was kind of fun, but goodbye.*

That is not what happens.
What happens is that the people you loved... still

love you. They will think of you. They will miss you every time a memory emerges. The gifts you gave will carry on the intentions of your spirit.

For me, Trung is more present now than ever before. When I turn on the car, holding the Texas keychain. When I am cold and end up wearing the jacket he gave me. Looking at a fourth motorcycle he convinced me I needed. Riding the Ducati 916 we bought together, or wearing the t-shirt he gave me, too tight and provocative for my age.

Your friends will still talk about you. Sharing the moments and the laugh you shared with them. People will still do things for you, and you will do things for them even if indirectly.

I came to think of Trung's passing as *simply* the temporary absence of his physical presence from my everyday life. As if the person is on a trip somewhere.

Beyond that, nothing is really different: Trung is still my brother – still funny, still crazy, but just away for a while.

Trung on the Ducati 916 at Laguna Seca Racetrack,
waving at the imaginary crowd of fans.

No worries T, I will catch up with you in no
time...

DARIO D'ANGELO

CHAPTER SIXTEEN

DIE, FOR HEAVENS SAKE!

To quote Alan Watts: "The Christian version of hell is as abominable as the Christian version of heaven… nobody wants to be in church forever."

Master Watts, I respectfully disagree. I think that if you belong to a religious belief – any religious belief – you are like Dorothy in Wonderland or Michael Jackson in Neverland. If anything, dying is the best thing that can happen to you.

The Christian heaven is for Christians a blast: the eternal glory of God upon you, the angels singing, trumpets playing, and the whole deal. I assume there are no professional sports there (although nothing is mentioned in the Bible about it), but you are going to know the results of all the games played at all times past, present and future… which would kind of spoil the fun of it anyway.

Dante and Beatrice gaze upon the highest heavens;
from Gustave Doré's illustrations in the *Divine Comedy*.

So if you don't mind crowds (all the billions who
died before you), or being with your most annoying-
but-nice relatives *forever*, heaven is the place to be,
and death is how you get there. Good crowd... not
my cup of tea, but hell, better than the alternative.

If you are a Buddhist, you not only have one heaven but several, depending on your career of choice! It is declared that a warrior who fights for good and dies for his or her duties will enter the realm of the "devas of passionate delight."

If you are an actor who makes audiences laugh, you will enter the realm of the "laughing devas."

Stephen Colbert, I would abandon Catholicism if I were you. Laughing devas sounds like fun!

But let's not forget one very important Buddhist heaven: the Trāyastrimśa. Trāyastrimśa is the second of the heavens of the Kāmadhātu, and the highest of the heavens that maintains a physical connection with the rest of the world. Trāyastrimśa is located on the peak of Sumeru, the central mountain of the world, at a height of 80,000 yojanas (a height sometimes equated to about 40,000 feet) and a total area of 80,000 yojanas square.

Plausible? No. The perfect place to spend your post-retirement millennia? Absolutely. Although I hope all the good Karma boys and girls can fit in 80,000 yojanas. With seven billion souls, at an optimistic 5% good-person-to-bad ratio, we are talking about 140,000,000 good guys. That is 1,750 souls per yojana. I don't know... sounds like it is going to be crowded.

It is the Islamic religion that is really onto something, especially if you are a guy. I hope you really appreciate this discussion because I am saying this risking my life. As you know, these guys appreciate jokes as much as O.J. Simpson appreciated his wife.

Jannah in the Qu'ran, verse 35 of Surah Al-Ra'd reads, *"The parable of the Garden which the righteous are promised! Beneath it flow rivers. Perpetual is the fruits thereof and the shade therein. Such is the End of the Righteous; and the end of the unbelievers is the Fire."*

So, let me say first, they really give you no choice. If you don't believe, fire! Ok, so I will believe, no questions asked. But for the sake of the conversation, let's go deeper and see what the heavens here have to offer.

After extensive research (typing "Islamic heaven" in Wikipedia), I can give you a good description.

Heaven is characterized primarily in physical terms as a place where every wish is immediately fulfilled. It's a bit of a paradox, as you can wish you never died. But this is not about logic as it is about an exercise of imagination, so let's play along.

Islamic texts describe immortal life in heaven as happy, without negative emotion. Those who dwell in heaven are said to wear costly apparel, partake in exquisite banquets, and recline on couches inlaid with gold or precious stones. Imagine it as a *Beverly Hills Housewives* show but without the endless drama involving solely each other's feelings.

Inhabitants will rejoice in the company of their parents, wives, and children.

What I like the most is that Islamic texts refer to

several levels of heaven. Yes, levels! And this was before Pac-Man! I won't dwell on the details, but depending on the good-deeds-to-bad-deeds ratio, you can get to a given level of heaven. The available slots are:

1. Firdaus or Paradise
2. 'Adn, Na'iim
3. Na'wa
4. Darussalaam
5. Daarul Muaqaamah
6. Al-Muqqamul
7. Amin & Khuldi.

In Islam, if one's good deeds outweigh one's sins then one may gain entrance to heaven. Conversely, if one's sins outweigh one's good deeds, one is sent to hell. *True story!* I am currently striving for *sins = (good deeds − 1)*. You gotta love it when your eternal future is decided by simple arithmetic.

The more good deeds one has performed, the higher the level of heaven one achieves. *The good news is that even the lowest level of heaven is one hundred times better than the greatest life on Earth!!!* So really, worse case scenario if you make it in, *you are gold*. I mean literally: palaces are built by angels for the occupants using solid gold.

The highest level is the seventh heaven, in which God can be seen and where anything is possible. *ANYTHING!*

I can't wait, and nor should any fundamentalist Islamic believer (possibly without self-exploding).

But I suspect they share Kenny Chesney's eternal wisdom in his song "Everybody Wants to Go to Heaven":

Everybody wants to go to heaven
Have a mansion high above the clouds,
Everybody wants to go to heaven
But nobody wants to go now

I conclude this chapter with one of the most realistic visions of heaven (and hell) I discovered, given by an old Zen proverb – or *Koan,* as they are called.

A famous soldier came to the master Hakuin and asked:
"Master, tell me: is there really a heaven and a hell?"
"Who are you?" asked Hakuin.
"I am a soldier of the great Emperor's personal guard."
"Nonsense!" said Hakuin. "What kind of emperor would have you around him? To me you look like a beggar!"

At this, the soldier started to rattle his big sword in anger.
"Oho!" said Hakuin. "So you have a sword! I'll wager it's much too dull to cut my head off!"

At this the soldier could not hold himself back. He drew his sword and threatened the master, who said: "Now you know half the answer! You are opening the gates of hell!"

The soldier drew back, sheathed his sword, and bowed. "Now you know the other half," said the master. "You have opened the gates of heaven."

CHAPTER SEVENTEEN

NO REALLY, WHERE DO YOU WANT TO BE BURIED?

Even feeling as weird as I can possibly feel in saying this, I need to say it: I've spent a considerable amount of time thinking about the question: w*here do I want to be buried?*

The idea of my body being in a non-reusable, non-recyclable and unreasonably expensive coffin (a Satin Cherry Solid Hardwood Casket would cost about $2,500 bananas), all suited up nicely (another $500) and waiting for the bacteria to eat my remains to the bone, did not sound too exciting.

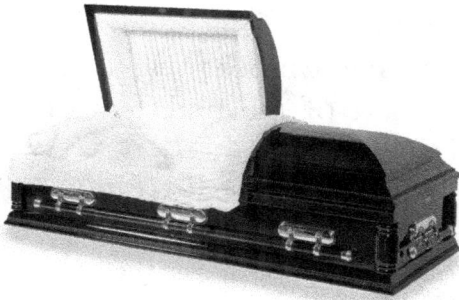

Top of the line model, solid wood, ready for… *use*. Air delivery, if you need it now. (Credit to *Dignified Caskets*)

So what are the alternatives? Cremation is one. That is: they burn you to ashes, and they grind your bones to dust. While I do appreciate the reduced environmental impact of my death and the lesser impact on my family's wallet[16], I am not too happy about this option either.

Put the ashes in an urn, on top of some relative's fireplace mantel, along with random knick-knacks and it gets somehow very creepy.

What happens in a bad economy.
(Credit: mainelyurns.com)

If they throw me in the ocean, I assume I will be fish food, which might not be too unfair, considering the thousands of fish I must have murdered during my lifetime. Un-poetic would be to become fish poop, or part of the undifferentiated mud at the bottom of the sea floor.

The sky route could be better if I can find

---

[16] If you are curious, I shopped around and you can get it done starting at $698. Cheap!

someone who would be willing to eject my remains from 3500 feet in the air. The problem is that I could very easily become the annoying dust that gets vacuum-cleaned once a year. So thanks, but no thanks.

How about being placed in the ground, let's say four to five feet deep with no coffin, in a forest or a sweeping grass field? Plant a seed of a beautiful tree just above me. Somehow I feel that nourishing the tree, slowly becoming part of it, and having it grow strong and healthy by using all the good nutrients I collected over so many years, is quite romantic and uplifting. *Giving back to the earth that raised me, and out of which I grew. Finally going back to be part of the world that made me.*

Pretty me, one day, sunbathing.
(Credit: miriadna.com)

The idea that in one form or another I will live in a tree is hopelessly romantic. Until I think about logging and deforestation, that is. But that is another book.

CHAPTER EIGHTEEN

CONCLUSION:
SO WHAT IS THE BRIGHT SIDE OF DEATH?

The answer to this question can not be simpler: *Life*. Does this really answer anything? Before you ask for your money back, read on.

I do believe that dying is not an end, but rather *a return* – a return to where we came from, the place where our bodies and minds are made. The beginning of a new cycle. The welcoming embrace of the earth and of the universe that created us.

The Enso in the image that follows, is an exercise of Japanese calligraphy used to express absolute enlightenment, strength, elegance, the universe, and the void. But to me it perfectly symbolizes a return to the origin.

An analogy that helps me wrap my thoughts around death and provides me a way to see it in a non-dramatic way, is to *observe* the "I" as the crest of a wave. The crest of the wave is part of the ocean, with individuality and expression, while still an interdependent entity. It's a unique manifestation of the ocean itself.

When a wave disappears, does it really die? No, not really. It goes back to its origin, to the very thing it was expressing. Is the wave lost forever? No, the very opposite: The wave was always there, part of the ocean, the exact place where it always will be.

And the ocean will express itself again. A new wave crest will rise and contemplate itself and its own nature, in a cycle that will never end.

(Credit: bostern.com)

This "I" might end; this "crest" might subside. But the circle of life will continue, and a new "I" will grow from this planet. There will be a heart like mine somewhere in this world, maybe without my memories, but with a sentience akin to mine.

Is there sadness in the loss of this "I"? Yes, there is. No one can ask us to pretend there is no pain in loss. But we need to appreciate the nature of this process and its context. If we look into the eyes of the pain, we will see there are all the reasons to move beyond this suffering.

I think now is a great time to get back to reality – to the *Eternal Now*, which is what we have, always have had, and indeed always will have.

THE END

(or is it? Yes, it is. I am kidding)

DARIO D'ANGELO

ABOUT THE AUTHOR

Dario D'Angelo was born in 1968 near Catania, an eastern city on the island of Sicily, Italy. Raised in Rome, he majored in Nuclear Energy at the ITIS E. Fermi, in Frascati. After two years in the military, he was hired by IBM Italy. Dario's interest in philosophy burgeoned from his endless conversations with his dear weight-lifting instructor, Francesco Candi, during his years of training for regional and national amateur competitions. In 1997, Dario left Italy to accept a position as Software Engineer at the IBM Silicon Valley Laboratory, CA and moved to the beautiful town of Los Gatos, where he happily lives with his wife and three cats. He maintains an abiding passion for science, innovation, and literature.